IMPRESSIONS OF THE BIG THICKET

NUMBER 4 BLAFFER SERIES OF SOUTHWESTERN ART

Morning sun through tall pines, Alabama-Coushatta Indian Reservation

IMPRESSIONS OF THE *Big Thicket*

Paintings by MICHAEL FRARY

Text by WILLIAM A. OWENS

FOREWORD BY JOHN PALMER LEEPER

UNIVERSITY OF TEXAS PRESS, AUSTIN AND LONDON

ACKNOWLEDGMENT

Although most of the paintings in this book were withheld by the artist from showings and sale until publication, a few have been purchased. The publisher wishes to thank the following owners for permitting their paintings to be included in this collection: Mr. and Mrs. Henry C. Beck (*Morning Sun through Tall Pines*); Mr. and Mrs. W. Terrell Blodgett (*Grape Vines on Dempsie's Island*); Mr. Raymond O. Johnson (*Scene near Saratoga*); Meredith Long Gallery (*Time of the Loon*); Mr. and Mrs. George Peterson (*Home of the Egret*); Miss Lucy Ross (*Paths Quickly Overgrown*); Mr. and Mrs. Charles Schmidt (*Slave Lake*); and Dr. H. Irving Schweppe, Jr. (*Egrets and White Herons*).

Library of Congress Cataloging in Publication Data

Frary, Michael, 1918–
  Impressions of the Big Thicket.

  (Blaffer series of southwestern art, no. 4)
  1. Big Thicket, Tex.—Description and travel—
Views. I. Owens, William A., 1905–   II. Title.
III. Series.
ND1839.F69083   917.64′14   73-1674
ISBN 0-292-70706-1

Printed in the United States of America
Composition by G&S Typesetters, Austin
Printing by Steck-Warlick Company, Austin
Binding by Universal Bookbindery, Inc., San Antonio

for KATE WILSON DAVIS, *who sees beauty in all of nature*

for LANCE ROSIER, *whose love for the Thicket was contagious*

for PEG FRARY, *whose faith, patience, and encouragement were boundless*

Contents

Foreword

Probably no area in the world has been depicted by artists so thoroughly as the North American continent; the unrolling of the great panorama has been witnessed by scores of capable and often inspired artists whose works held, and continue to hold, their admirers spellbound.

Artists through the centuries have traveled and lovingly recorded their impressions: Corot in Italy, Chinnery in China, Lear in Greece; but no land so consistently has beguiled artists as the Americas, and in particular the United States. The natural wonders of Niagara, of Yosemite, and such epochal movements as the conquest of the great plains have been documented as exhaustively in pigment as in words. This personal depiction is an authentic and enduring tradition in our art.

In the best instances the artists were painting from the inside out, as it were, rather than simply recording the novel or the spectacular. George Catlin and Alfred Jacob Miller, for example, not only were authorities on the American Indian, but also were deeply sympathetic to their subjects and attuned to them. This blending of understanding and harmony is the source of the particular poignancy and immediacy that pervades their work.

William A. Owens tells us of Michael Frary's introduction to the Big Thicket, and of his natural, intuitive response to its people and its ambiance. His were the right eye and brush and heart for the Big Thicket. The eye was right, for Frary's is a sensitive eye, quick to isolate the dramatic and enlarge upon it. He looks upward into the branches of a dead cypress and sees its compelling pattern; a strong sense of design has always been characteristic of his work. He takes in everything: the watercolors of the Thicket are encyclopaedic in their range of shapes and colors, of leaves and flowers, of reflections and dark waters. The walls of trees become tapestries of saturated greens flecked with blues. Meticulously painted herons step cautiously and elegantly before them.

The brush of Mike Frary is an immensely skillful one, as his distinguished career attests. He is a virile painter, working with decision and bravura; the vocabulary of brush strokes is endless, appropriate to the profusion of textures and colors at hand. The physical quality of his painting never flags, and one is aware of the speed and intensity with which he works. Nothing is omitted; the stops are out; and one is enveloped in this luxuriant, mysterious world painted without restraint or hesitation.

But, most significantly, the heart of Michael Frary is right for this project, and he was attuned to it. In his best work Frary is a natural painter, and the more immediate he is to the subject and the painting, the more powerful he becomes. Despite the adroit, well-organized canvases he has produced, he becomes vibrant when he is responding directly. There are no theories here; he is expressive, not analytical, and we are moved.

Michael Frary was born in Santa Monica, California, and spent his youth in Florida, graduating from the West Palm Beach High School. He returned to California to study at the University of Southern California, from which he received a Bachelor of Architecture degree in 1940, and the Master of Fine Arts degree in painting the following year. Despite many excursions elsewhere, Frary has always been primarily oriented to the broad axis of southern United States, and in his watercolors and oil paintings he has recorded its beaches, its vegetation, its sun-filled and wind-swept landscapes. Notably, both in Florida and during college, Frary was a champion swimmer and water-polo player, mastering the natural, even indigenous sports of the regions.

Following his discharge from the United States Navy in 1945, Frary was an art director for the Goldwyn, Paramount, and Universal studios. He has been indefatigable as an artist, taking advantage of every professional opportunity and participating fully in the immediate art affairs. Wherever he has been, he has taught—at the University of Southern California, in Missouri, in Colorado —during summers as well as the school year. It was teaching that brought him to Texas originally. Dorothy Blodgett records that the late Dalzell Hatfield of the Hatfield Galleries in Los Angeles first introduced Frary to Texas. Hatfield had close interests in San Antonio, for he was profoundly instrumental in the formation of the collection of Marion Koogler McNay there and in the ultimate creation of the museum of modern art that bears her name. Frary first taught at the San Antonio Art Institute, and in 1952 he accepted a position with the University of Texas, which named him professor of art in 1970. It was an easy, harmonious transfer from California to Texas, and the artist was immediately at home, easily absorbing the state's traditions and manners.

Perhaps more than any artist in Texas, Michael Frary has been a responsible participant in its art scene. For example, he has consistently submitted paintings to juried exhibitions, year after year, when many of his fellow artists felt they had grown beyond them. The submission of a painting is much more than that simple act. It is the artist's recognition of the importance of the exhibition, however small, of the effort behind it. He is offering his support at a time when he is more apt to be concerned with his national or international reputation, at a time when regional art is declared nonexistent or, if it happens to linger, not important.

"Regional art" is in disfavor today, for it is thought to be stylistically confining and idiosyncratic. Actually, it is valid and important, often bespeaking an affectionate, even passionate understanding of a region by an artist.

The results of Frary's warm-hearted participation have been twofold: first, an unrivaled list of awards and one-man exhibitions. His special commissions and representation in public and private collections have followed apace. The second result has been the production of an enormous corpus of painting in which he has explored his own reactions, formulated his own philosophies. He is thus highly articulate as an artist, and there is nothing diffident or taciturn in his statements.

Other artists of the area have dwelt on its pensive and nostalgic aspects. None, however, have caught its excitement and splendor so forcefully. Michael Frary is indeed equipped with the trained eye, the skilled brush, and the responsive heart for which the Big Thicket called.

JOHN PALMER LEEPER

IMPRESSIONS OF THE BIG THICKET

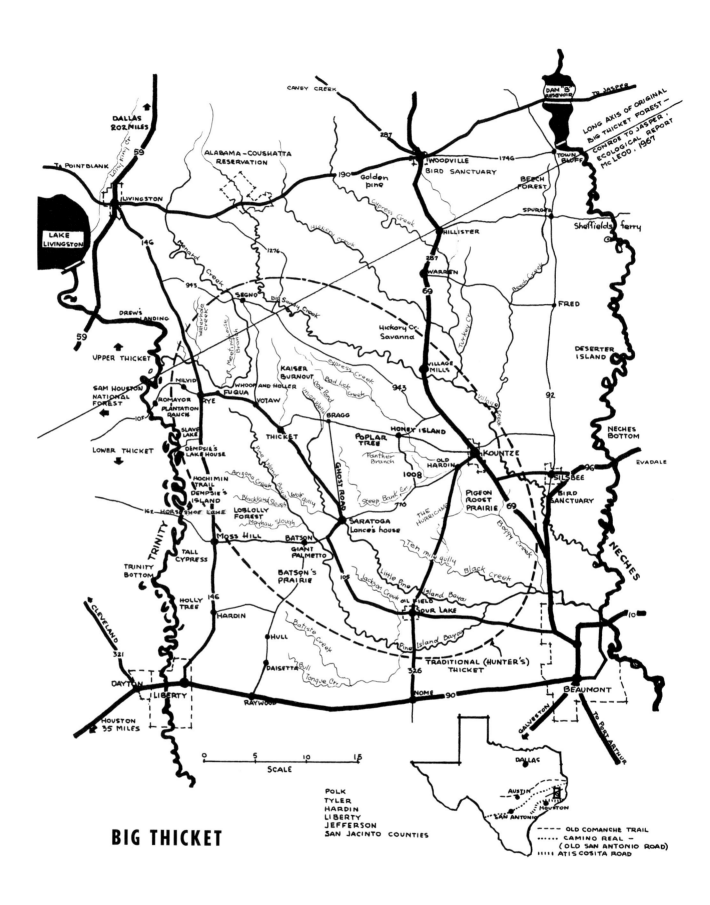

BIG THICKET

POLK
TYLER
HARDIN
LIBERTY
JEFFERSON
SAN JACINTO COUNTIES

LONG AXIS OF ORIGINAL
BIG THICKET FOREST:
CONROE TO JASPER.
ECOLOGICAL REPORT:
McLEOD, 1967

--- OLD COMANCHE TRAIL
..... CAMINO REAL —
(OLD SAN ANTONIO ROAD)
IIIII ATIS COSITA ROAD

SCALE

Big Thicket Patterns AN ESSAY

My love affair with the Big Thicket began in June, 1933, when I was on my way to Port Arthur to become a learner in the S. H. Kress and Company store. I left Dallas on a Sunday night with the conductor my only companion in the coach. Toward midnight he got out two lengths of twelve-inch board, unvarnished but well polished from use, laid them across two seats, and spread a blanket over them. This was my bed for the night. Before morning we would travel on tracks of what was once the Houston East and West Texas, derisively called the "Hell Either Way You Take It." Before morning we would cross into what the conductor called "deep East Texas," north of Beaumont, which is fourteen miles north of Port Arthur.

When I woke up we were crawling through a dense forest with a wall of trees on either side that came up close to the track. The sun was up but visible only as glints of light on bark and leaf where the greens of the upper canopy met the bright blue of the sky. Nearer the earth the lower canopy was a tangle of bush and vine and Spanish moss, a place of shadows where the sun rarely penetrated. The smell of coal smoke drifted through the open windows, a smell that grew fainter as it mingled with the smell of wet woodland and of flowers, some too sweet, some overripe.

Still more than a hour out of Beaumont, I rode the back platform, feeling almost close enough to branch and flower to touch with an outstretched hand. Pines, oaks, sweetgums made an

ever-changing pattern, with here and there the glossy green leaves and waxy white flowers of magnolias lifting toward the sun. There was water in the borrow pits along the roadbed and at times we passed swamps where palmettos crowded half-train high, or where cypress trees thrust black branches above clinging gray moss.

Even from the train platform I could see enough variety of trees and plants and flowers, of dappled glade and murky swamp, to know that I was witness to unusual minglings of nature. I was unaware then, as too many Americans—indeed, too many Texans—are still, that the coming together of plants, animals, and birds, some of them rare, makes the Big Thicket as unique as the Everglades or other better-known natural phenomena. Also, I was unaware that conservationists were already at work trying to save it from and for the people living and working there.

For the first long stretch I saw neither houses nor people. I watched when the train whistled for crossings and saw some wagon roads, some logging roads, but could not tell where they went, they were so soon out of sight in the thickets. People were back in there, I knew. People lived back in there. I did not see their houses but I did see their scrubby cattle and razorback hogs—their woods rooters—on the right-of-way. There was no stock law there, the conductor told me. Sometimes the train had to stop while the crew took an animal off the cowcatcher.

We came out of the thickets and, after Beaumont, onto the coastal plain for the short distance to Port Arthur and the broad expanse of Lake Sabine, the "dreening" place for much of the region. From the platform of a train I had seen a part of the Big Thicket. From what I had seen it was strange enough, in its darker stretches mysterious enough, to make me want to go back.

The wish was strengthened by a writer I met in Port Arthur, Ethel Osborn Hill, who for years had been studying the flora and fauna and people—especially the people—of the Big Thicket and was, as I learned later, partly a product of the Thicket. While we were talking on her back porch an oversized cockroach came out of the dark and started across the floor. Without pausing in her conversation she took off a shoe and smashed him with the heel, starting a cockroach-killing game which livened a conversation that needed no livening. With songs and stories she told me about the pineys and the swampers and the feuds among them. From her I heard the first time of that unusual mixture in the Thicket of white, Indian, and Negro, called there the Red Bones. She impressed on me the independence of spirit of Thicket people and their dislike of outsiders—especially of anyone who might turn out to be a "revenooer" in search of stills and corn whiskey. One story I remember vividly. Two

men were feuding over some corn—over one man's hogs in another man's corn, I believe. One of them, the survivor, told how the feud ended: "He tried to put on me and I wan't gonna be put on, so I shot him." The talk turned from people to plants. She was the first to tell me about the insect-eating pitcher plant and the uses of sweet myrtle. In the Big Thicket a branch of myrtle on the front gate was a sign of sickness or other trouble inside the house, a plea for the passerby to stop and help. Before our visit was over I knew that, drawn as I was to the study of folklore, I had to have a closer look at this land, these people.

Almost five years passed before I could get back. This time I carried an old recording machine that embossed the sounds of ballads and fiddle tunes on aluminum discs. By this time I was an instructor in English at Texas Agricultural and Mechanical College and deeply involved in collecting Texas folklore and writing about Texas people. The man in the dormitory room next to mine was Larry J. Fisher, who had spent a great deal of time around Saratoga, near the heart of the Big Thicket. He had an extensive collection of photographs he had made of scenes, plants, and people; he had written plays about historical events in which he had tried to recapture the individuality of the people and the romance of the land. At the time, he was writing *The Kaiser Burnout*, a play based on a Civil War incident, about which there is a great deal of folklore but not much verifiable detail, if any.

When Texas seceded from the Union, not all were in favor, including Sam Houston. As in other areas, especially border areas, along with the development of the regular Union Army and the Confederate Army there were organizations of guerrilla bands, the proslavery called bushwhackers, the antislavery called jayhawkers. Some of the Big Thicket residents, wanting no part of a war that did not seem to affect them, withdrew into Hardin County thickets, not so much as a guerrilla band but as a group loosely organized for self-protection, though the name jayhawkers was given them. Not bushwhackers but a unit of the Confederate Army tried to bring them out, but without success. According to legend, in 1865 Captain James Kaiser was

sent from Galveston to Woodville with a small detachment. His decision at the last was to burn them out, and he did, at the cost of an unknown number of lives and acres and acres of virgin forest. Out of all the folklore two things are certain: the burned-out area still appears burned out and the legends around the incident have done much to define the independence of the Big Thicket character and, through many tellings, to create it.

Unfinished though it was at the time, Larry's play gave considerable insight into patterns of Big Thicket life and ways of thinking. From him I learned much, but I still had to go see for myself.

This time, late winter hung on. Branches of oaks, beeches, maples, and gums were bare. Exposed to the light were the dense thickets of holly called yaupon with gray-green leaves and clear red berries, of bright green smilax climbing high on bare branches and tumbling back on lower bushes, of low growing banks of fragrant sweet myrtle, of magnolias and bays tall and spreading where they had made room for themselves to grow.

For my purposes I had one of the best guides to the Thicket, Irvin (Cocky) Thompson, whose son Houston was a student friend at Texas A&M. Cocky knew the paved roads that crossed it, the wagon roads barely passable for a car, the trails that led to log cabins or became lost in the rootings of hogs searching for mast. He knew the people and where to find them. Through the depression he had peddled Watkins liniment in and around Silsbee, and as deep into the Thicket as he could go by buggy or on horseback. Thicket people trusted him enough to let him know who was moonshining and where the stills could be found. They knew he was not a revenue man, and, some said, too much against the law himself to turn them in. He could holler at almost any gate and be told to come on in—"to set by the fire" or to swig from a jug on the mantelpiece "something stronger'n Watkins liniment." Because I was with him I was also asked in and howdyed, usually with three questions: "What's yer name?" "Whar did you come from?" "You got any kinfolks around here?" The last was sometimes answered by an old man or an old woman who would look at me a long time and say, "I don't recollect the favor"—a way of saying that my face did not call to mind a family resemblance.

I in turn put together what information I could get from those willing to talk and especially those willing to sing me a "ballet" or play me a tune. I wanted to know who they were: Where they were born, when they were born, how long they had lived where they were living. I also wanted to know who their parents were and where they had come from. From time to time I asked whether they considered themselves residents

of the Big Thicket. More often than not the answer was negative; by too many the Big Thicket was thought to be the worst part of the backwoods. Many of them told me I would find it "down yan ways a piece."

Cocky Thompson smiled at them, too understanding of their feelings to contradict them. Then he undertook to show me what he understood to be the Big Thicket, as well as more of the people. From Silsbee we traveled east to Evadale on the Neches River, where we sat on a houseboat with a fisherman's family, the children yellowed with malaria, and listened to stories of big mud cats and six-foot gars caught, of alligators now and then lazing in the yellow water, and to the whangy singing of ancient ballads of lords and ladies in England, "somewheres across the waters."

North we went to Fred, skirting on the way miles of swamp with low-growing vegetation, sparsely settled, the people we saw on the roads looking worn down, bedraggled, people called "swampers" by their neighbors. We continued north as far as Spurger, into the knolls and rolling hills, covered with open pine forests, more thickly settled, more prosperous looking, though there were log and plank houses with see-through cracks, homes of "pineys."

By woods roads we went as far west as Village Mills, southwest to Votaw, and then by more open roads back to Silsbee by way of Saratoga and Kountze, having covered in our journeys parts of Hardin, Tyler, and Polk counties, the areas of his youth. Without him to point out occasional denseness on one side or the other, I could have traveled the main roads up and down without knowing I was in the Thicket; but then he took me on sandy roads to settlements or single houses deep in the woods, on logging roads worn down by lumber companies half a century earlier or more, on corduroy roads of logs laid in mud by oil drillers and pipeliners. When roads ran out, we went on foot along trails where generations of Thicketers had hunted for deer at night with, before flashlights, a flaming "light'd knot" of pitch pine to shine their eyes.

Between Votaw and Saratoga we explored the outer edge of a baygall, which he called "begall," a swampy, watery blemish on the earth where trees grew high above the underbrush and vines big as your leg looped low over green-brown water. Near Kountze we toured "Pigeon Roost Prairie." According to him, pigeons in passage stopped here in such great numbers that they broke down trees and overfertilized the ground till trees would not grow again. This could be another folk tale, as there are other prairies—grassy spaces—in the Thicket. There are still enough birds—but not pigeons—there to make the story almost plausible.

Cocky's lessons were good but, as I learned later, they covered only a part of what was originally called the Big Thicket, the lower part, the part that now contains most of what is left. Early scouts thought that, north to south, it reached from the Old San Antonio Road, the Camino Real, from where it crossed the Sabine at Gaines Ferry, near San Augustine, to the coastal plain near Beaumont and, east to west, along the Camino Real from the Sabine to the Brazos River. Before long, they realized that the Trinity River formed the western boundary. The southern boundary followed roughly the line of the coastal plain from Beaumont to Liberty, near the mouth of the Trinity. Even with these limitations, it included some three million acres spread over all or part of eleven counties. By 1938 it had dwindled to about a million acres. Inroads on the remainder were visible from almost any direction—in paved highways, towns, villages, sawmills, and oil derricks. Conversely, some land was being put into tree farms, some too worn out for farming was being allowed to return to its natural growth.

Historically, the Big Thicket can be said to have been bounded on the east by the Neutral Ground. After the Louisiana Purchase, the United States and Spain were unable to agree on a boundary between Louisiana and Texas. In 1806 they agreed that the disputed area between the Arroyo Hondo on the east and the Sabine on the west would remain neutral, with no settlers allowed. It soon became a refuge for outlaws, horse thieves, gamblers, and runaway slaves, a population so lawless that military expeditions had to be mounted against them in the period from 1810 to 1812. When the United States acquired ownership in 1821 the area was cleared of some of the more notorious, but the bad reputation was already well established. Some of those driven out crossed into the Big Thicket, not as settlers but as fugitives, bad men.

At the same time, settlers were beginning to arrive, drawn by the policy of the Mexican government to grant good land at cheap prices, or by the hope of being able to squat on land long enough to claim it as their own. At first the migration formed two streams: Those from the lower South followed the coastal plain, those from the upper South followed the open forested hilly land through Arkansas and northern Louisiana. The Big

Thicket lay between. They came in such increasing numbers that in 1836, the year of Texas independence, four Big Thicket counties were formed: Jasper, Liberty, Sabine, and San Augustine. Accurate surveying was impossible. Indeed, boundaries between some of these counties remain indefinite because of the denseness of thickets, the inaccessibility of swamps and sluggish streams.

Though I talked to anyone who could tell me about the Big Thicket, I sought out first the ones living in isolated settlements or in houses off the main roads. As we talked, a general character began to be clear, a character not too different from that to be found in any of the Southern mountain or lowland states, coming as it did from essentially the same stock. Most of the early settlers in East Texas were descended from the English, Scotch-Irish, and Welsh who had populated Virginia and the Carolinas and by the time of the Revolutionary War had moved westward as far as Kentucky. As new territory opened up they flowed in great numbers into Georgia and then on to Alabama, Mississippi, Arkansas, Louisiana, and Texas, bringing with them the language, lore, and Calvinistic beliefs which were perpetuated as much in Big Thicket settlements as in lonely valleys in the Southern Appalachians. The few who owned slaves brought them. Most were poor whites who came by oxcart and brought with them only the tools to build log houses and clear land for crops.

Much of the land they found, especially in the upper part, was like the land they had left in Tennessee, Alabama, and northern Mississippi—sandy, wooded, slightly rolling, good for the kinds of crops a man with the help of his wife and children could farm: cotton, corn, sweet potatoes, and several kinds of garden "sass." Groups came together and settled together where there was good land, good water, good timber a-plenty, and game to be had for the taking. For the most part they settled first in the upper Thicket or on the edges where scenes were familiar. Other parts they considered mysterious—the mystery explainable by the deep silences of wood and water, the legends of people hiding there, the cry of a panther like a woman screaming in the night.

As there was no electricity in the settlements to power a recording machine, I had to depend for songs and stories on people who had moved to town, or who were willing to go to town on the promise of a chance to hear their own voices—like being on the radio. My first session, by good luck and Cocky's arranging, was at the home of Ben Hooks in Kountze on a Saturday night too foggy for hunting. Ben and his brother Bud were fiddlers and they had brought in a young man to second on the guitar. They were eager to hear themselves but they were patient while I got some of the notes I needed.

In many ways they and their family had lived Big Thicket history for two generations. Their parents had come in a covered wagon from Georgia in 1849; two of the brothers had served in the Confederate Army; they themselves had been a part of the oil boom that hit Sour Lake, Batson's Prairie, and Saratoga. They were widely known as hunters—as widely known for shooting it out in a Big Thicket shooting scrape.

Ben's house was white frame and comfortable but it did not advertise the wealth they held in land and timber and oil leases. From their clothes, they might have been hired hands, but not from their faces when they got tuned up and, in East Texas language, "showered down" on a piece. They were white-haired men then, probably in their seventies, but there was youth in the nimbleness of finger and twinkle of eye. Their tunes, though they did not say so then, reached back through the history of the migration that finally settled them in the Big Thicket. There was the cloggy beat of "The Irish Washerwoman" and a graceful lilt in "The Rustic Dance" reminiscent of Scotland. From the trek across the American frontier there was "Leather Britches" and close to the Thicket itself "Cattle in the Canebrake." Roughness of life on the Mississippi echoed in "Natchez under the Hill." The breaking away of slave from master, the conflicts of the Civil War, became wryly humorous in "Run, nigger, run, the paterollers'll git you. . . . Run, nigger, run, it's almost day." Between the fiddle pieces there was some talk of old times, but I did not know enough to ask the right questions. The opportunity never came again.

I expected my research to be chiefly among descendants of the Anglo-Saxon pioneers. Nevertheless, I was eager to learn what I could in the Negro settlements on the edges of white towns. The next night I was at a small Baptist church in Silsbee recording, among others, descendants of slaves brought to Texas a hundred years earlier: men who worked in lumber mills or timber, women who "he'ped out" in white folks' kitchens for a dollar or two a week and daily "totin's."

The church was close inside, dimly lit, and the wood floor was like a sounding board for rough shoes keeping time. There were solos, quartets, congregational singing. The songs were spiritual, Gospel, expanded to include human experience, work experience, which seemed much the same whether they were slave or free:

> Through the years I keep on toiling,
> Toiling through sunshine and rain.

Hope in this one only in "patiently waiting till my Savior comes again."

To me the most poignant of all was sung by a frail black woman who carried "warshing and arning" through town in bundles on her head:

> Sometimes I'm up, sometimes I'm down,
> I'm going to lay down this heavy load;
> Sometimes I'm almost to the ground,
> I'm going to lay down this heavy load.

In lumber camps I found blues and other kinds of songs—what the preachers called "sinful songs"—which told the Negro experience sometimes humorously, sometimes angrily, but always with feeling. In a home in the Negro section of Silsbee I recorded an old black man singing a song with a fairly typical mixture of nonsense, blasphemy, and satire:

> Preacher in the henhouse on his knees,
> Oh, mona,
> Thought he heard a chicken sneeze,
> Oh, mona;
> Sneezed so hard with the whooping cough,
> Oh, mona,
> Sneezed his head and his tail right off,
> Oh, mona, you shall be free when the good Lord
>   sets you free.

This same old man, who could neither read nor write, whose knees were bowed by heavy work in the timber, sang a love lament that opened with the improbable lines:

> Something's come between us;
> I'm about to lose my Venus.

No one could tell me where this song came from, or who brought it to the Thicket, or whether it was remembered outside the Thicket. In the minstrel world, from which it may have come, whites blacked up like blacks and sang imitation black songs, but there was no real meeting of their cultures. In the Big Thicket it was clear that the two cultures—black and white —existed side by side with many overlappings and many borrowings one from the other.

For a time I thought there might be overlappings from a third —the Indian—but in my initial explorations I was disappointed. The Alabama-Coushatta Indian Reservation was established in

Polk County, near Livingston, before the Civil War and had been in existence a century at the time of my first visit. Under the shade of trees and of tin-roofed houses I found old men who grudgingly talked to me, but I found no one who could, or would, tell me Indian stories or sing me Indian songs, though others have had somewhat better luck in later years. They did show me a bare sand graveyard, the graves decorated with coal oil lamps and china dishes, the children's graves pathetic with dolls and toys fading in the broiling sun. At a kind of commissary they had baskets for sale—small baskets exquisitely woven from fine marsh grass. Eagerly I looked among them for one with an Indian design. There was none. The only ones with a design at all had GOD IS LOVE worked in brown straw on white. The white man's preacher had educated them away from what was their own. What I had found was not overlapping of cultures each on the other but the imposition of one on the other. Frustrated, feeling somewhat the intruder, I turned back to the predominant—the Anglo-Saxon.

The depression still hung on. Times were hard, food scarce. Game was not as plentiful in the Thicket as it had been, though deer could still be found, and near Livingston the children refused to go to school till a bear was hunted out and killed. "Woods rooter" hogs became a chief source of meat and conflict. They needed as wide a range as possible for gathering roots and mast, and for multiplying. Unmarked, they looked alike and a man might shoot somebody else's thinking it was his own, especially when meat was scarce. Stock laws were optional. Conflict between people trying to raise gardens and crops and owners of hogs and cattle was inevitable. Even in Silsbee there was no stock law. Hungry hogs rooted in flower yards and gardens and overturned vegetable stands outside grocery stores. Only when tempers ran out of control was a stock law passed. Even then, the argument that it was cheaper to fence out than to fence in prevailed in most of the area.

Armadillos, moving north and east at the time in great numbers, provided a source of meat for those who could stomach them, and quite a few confessed they could. At one home I visited, there was a smokehouse hung with dressed armadillos and a hickory fire going. The man told me that, smoked, they tasted something like pork and were just as filling. Like their pioneer ancestors, Thicketers had learned to live on what the land provided. If it was only armadillos, they could live on them, fixed up a little with pepper sauce and eased down with turnip greens and black-eyed peas.

I heard many stories of violence but the people, when I met them and overcame their distrust of an outsider, seemed no more violent than those on any other part of the American frontier. Rather, they were quiet and polite and at times shy. There were verifiable stories of feuds and murder. There were others that seemed to have no origin in fact. Probably, in the hundred years or so of isolation, their stories had been retold many times, added to in the retelling, even multiplied in their progress from settlement to settlement.

There was the old fiddler on the road above Fred. Several people made him out to be a bad man and a good fiddler. One person I interviewed was direct when he warned me not to go see him: "He's kilt four men and he ain't a-feard o' killing an-other'n." When I did go to see him, on a hot summer morning, he was on the front porch with his wife and a neighbor man. All three were probably in their fifties, though they were made to look older by brown leathery faces and stooped shoulders. The house was boarded and stripped and had only a front porch, what they called the big room, and a shed room at the back. There was no ceiling and a saddle hung astride a rafter on the porch.

For a time I did most of the talking. Then, when they had become a little friendly, I asked him about fiddling. Yes, he played a little but nothing to brag about. He sometimes played for dances when no other fiddler would come. He was a God-fearing man but he could see no harm in folks getting together for some fiddling and dancing. No worse'n going to some of them old Josie parties. He was not the first Thicketer I had talked to who thought it might be just as sinful to dance to somebody singing "Hold my mule while I dance Josie" as to somebody fiddling it.

Then he was willing to saw a tune for me. We went inside and he took his fiddle from a case under the bed. After rosining his bow, tuning to his ear, and trying some double stops, he played several tunes, including "Soldier's Joy," "Eighth of January," also called "The Battle of New Orleans," and "Billy in the Low Ground." Then he began recalling the days of his youth when he rode horseback all up and down the country to play the fiddle at dances. Sometimes, when the young people "bagged," as he pronounced begged, till they couldn't say no, he and his wife gave dances at their house. Man alive, the people poured in.

"One night," he said, "so many folks crowded in we didn't have room for fiddling and dancing, too." He looked up at the rough twelve-by-two joists. "We put the fiddlers up there. We clomb up there and set a-straddle where we was out'n the way o' the dancing. You never in your life heered sich fiddling and stomping. It purt nigh lasted all night."

Before the morning was over I asked him if he would go with me to find electricity to run the recording machine and record his music. He reckoned he could not do that. He was used to

staying around his place and I would find better fiddlers closer to town. Afraid of making him feel put on, I went on my way without insisting. He may have been a killer. I never knew, and, after my visit with him, did not want to find out.

During my years of going into the Thicket I felt threatened only once and that was at a house back toward the Neches, not far from Deserter Island. People said that Red Bones lived there and that they had come from somewhere over in Louisiana, maybe around Natchitoches. People said they were unfriendly, but, after the rumors and folklore I had heard about Red Bones, I wanted to find out what I could for myself. Once in Port Arthur I had seen a girl from up in the Thicket who was called a Red Bone. She was young and lithe and supple under the green silk of her dress. Her hair was red and curly, her skin a dark ivory. The green of her eyes was heightened by the emerald of her dress. She was striking enough in appearance to make me curious about the people she came from. Now, I thought, there was a chance.

The house, built of pine poles, was set in a low place and sheltered by low-growing liveoaks hung with Spanish moss. As I walked up to the front gate a man, woman, and several children came to the porch. They had black, Indian-straight hair, black eyes, and malaria-mud skins. The man spoke to me and there was a foreign Frenchy sound in his voice.

"You look for something?"

I asked for his name but did not get it. There was hostility in his evasions, in the way he shook his head. When I tried to tell him my business—making records of them that would sound like the radio—he turned his back on me angrily and went inside. The others followed him. They may have thought I was the law; they may simply have been suspicious of me as an outsider; it could be they had never heard of a radio. In any case, they made it clear that they wanted me to leave, and I could feel them watching me all the way back to the car. Rumors of Red Bones still persist. I have no proof of ever having encountered one.

In 1941 I took a job with the University of Texas collecting and recording folklore. Though my work required traveling over most of the state, I kept returning to the Big Thicket, partly because I could still find there people singularly untouched by highways and cars rushing by, or by any kind of communication with the outside world. There was still a reservoir of archaic language and song; there was still a frontier and links to earlier frontiers all the way back to England, Scotland, Ireland. I could begin to sense an almost palpable effect of Big Thicket living.

Though war and rumblings of war were beginning to bring

better times to other parts of the country, the depression still hung on in the Big Thicket. Life was hard; long lines still formed where surplus commodities were given out for relief. Government workers, many of them untrained, surviving on created jobs, tried to help a few of the people.

At Sandy Creek settlement, near Fred, where the Popes and Drydens—including a John Dryden—lived, the government set up a night school for adults in the schoolhouse and put in charge a man who had no training as a teacher but who had been given a government job. Monday night, because he did not know how to begin teaching people with so little education—many of whom could not read or write—he took along a portable radio and let them listen to it. Many had never before heard a radio. When time came for lessons they refused to listen to anything but the radio. Tuesday night it was the same. And Wednesday and Thursday. Ironically, on Friday some bureaucrat ordered the school closed because the people were not learning anything.

A WPA employee in Woodville offered to guide me through parts of the Thicket I had not seen before. The day was steamy hot with a bright sun overhead and no breath stirring in the walled growth on either side of the wagon road we were traveling. Suddenly we came upon a house that demonstrated clearly the ingenuity of Big Thicket people. It was a usual log house with the usual stick-and-dirt chimney at one end. The difference was that, in an area where heavy rainfall might be expected to wash the chimney away in a short time, the builder had added overhanging eaves which protected the chimney and gave the house a distinctly modern look.

Eager to get a picture of the house to take back to Austin, I stopped, helloed till the people came out—among them a very pretty girl about eighteen and barefoot—and told them why I had stopped. They agreed for me to take a picture of the house but they wanted the girl in it. That was acceptable to me, but then a problem arose. The girl had no shoes and it was not fitten for a gal as big as she was to have her picture made barefooted. In the midst of the discussion she turned to me and said, "C'n I borry your shoes to have my picture made?"

I took off my heavy crepe-soled low-quarters. She put them on, posed for the picture, and gave them back.

Everyone was happy. When we drove away they were calling to us, "You'uns come back to see us when you c'n."

A storekeeper near Fred told a story of an old woman who walked in out of the thickets one morning and came to the store.

"You got any wire pinchers?" she asked.

He brought out his pliers and handed them to her.

"You want to borry them?"

She shook her head and pointed to a swelling on her cheek.

"I got this tooth that's hurting me so it's got to be pulled. I'd be obliged if you'd take them pinchers and pull it."

She straddled a board sticking out from the porch floor, locked her arms and legs around it, and lifted her head with her mouth open wide enough for him to see the tooth and the swelling around it. He told her that he had no medicine to kill pain or prevent blood poisoning. She told him to pull.

He fastened the pliers on the tooth and yanked it out. She spat out a mouthful of blood and said, "I thank you."

Then she put her finger in her mouth and rested it on a tooth that to him looked sound.

"That'n might git to hurting me," she said. "You c'n pull it while you're a-pulling. It'd keep me from having to come back."

He pulled the tooth. Again she stood it without wince or whimper. Then she poured a box lid of snuff under her lower lip and headed back into the thickets.

On one of my trips in 1941 I found Rod Drake, who in his life history, his language, and his recollections of folklore was Big Thicket through and through. "I was borned in Tyler County in 1883," he said. "My father was borned in Texas. My mother come from Georgy in a oxcart when she was about five years old." He was a collector of songs and stories because he liked them. He had little interest in where they came from, or who brought them. He could vaguely reckon time back as far as the Civil War—"the old war," he called it—but he was no help when I tried to trace songs with him back through Southern mountains and valleys, or farther back to English, Scottish, Irish origins. When I recorded him, in 1952, his mind was clear, his memory phenomenal.

His schooling, as he described it, was not very different from that of more than a score of others I interviewed:

When I first went to school I was quite small. You know, a long time ago they didn't have but about three months o' school. And we lived up here close to Fred. I went to a school called Shiloh. Just one little old room. A little old shotgun house. And there's where I went the most of my time till I got to be about eighteen years old. After I got to be eighteen years old I had a cousin that was teaching school at what they call Caney Head up here on the Neches River about twenty-five miles above Silsbee, and he told me if I'd go and stay with him and just help him out every evening he'd give me a good education. So I started going to school to him when I was about eighteen years old. I managed to git about three months schooling there and I got a girl on my mind, and I left with the girl away from school and I never did git no more education.

Like other Big Thicket boys, he could work around his family's place or get a job in the timber:

When I was a young man I was raised up with lots of cattle. My father had lots of cattle and I used to break yearlings and raise and work them. That's the way we hauled our cotton and stuff, you know. There was a fellow named Brown who lived up here above Silsbee and he was a contractor hauling logs, snaking them over there for the Silsbee people. And he was putting them there by the old Silsbee camp near the train. And he said if I'd come over he'd give me a job. I had never hauled no logs before. I was a stout young man about twenty years old and I went over there. He wanted to give me three old steers and a log cart and wanted me to haul logs, and I told him, "Well, I ain't never hauled no logs but I'll try it." So I takened the job and I went to work and it come just as natural for me to drive them oxens as it did anything else, and I worked there with him a long time.

In the more thickly settled parts of the Thicket singing school was as important in the summer as regular school was in the winter. Singing masters went from settlement to settlement teaching the rudiments of music: reading shaped notes, marking time, "sol fa-ing" if Sacred Harp books were used, and singing a part in four-part harmony. Rod Drake told of his chance to get this kind of training:

During the time I was there I used to sing a lot and I had a friend working there, too, by the name of Phelps. Me'n him used to stay together when we was boys and both of us used to sing together a whole lot, and I got to singing out there one day and Brown told me, he said, "Rod, I'll tell you what I'll do," says, "if you'll go to singing school and take an interest in it and learn to sing," says, "I'll pay your way." You know, I never would do it. I just worked on there till I got tired and quit. If I'd a went on at the time I could have been worth something, but I just never did do it. I never did take no interest in nothing but just these old foolish songs like I'm singing now. Of course, I went to church and sang in church, but I never did practice none, and that was what he wanted me to do. He wanted me to go and learn to be a singer, but I was just an old boy then and didn't care.

These "old fool songs" provided both romance and drama for backwoods people who had few books and little else other than the Bible to meet these needs. They could be equally a part of life for a lonesome singer or for a group come together to pass the time. For Rod Drake, as well as for others, they were a part of courtship:

When I was a young man my father lived a way up in Tyler County on the west side of Beech Creek, back in the backwoods kinda, and I had a girl lived way down the creek below me and I had to cross the creek to go to see her. Very often the creek would get to swimming a horse, and I don't know how many times I swum that creek going down to see her, and I courted that girl a little better than five years before me and her married. I'd usually go to see her in the morning part of the day and I'd stay with her till late at night, and then I'd start back home, and I'd git on my horse there and I'd ride to where I lived, and I'd sing all the way, and she could hear me for a mile after I left there. When I'd go back to her the next time she'd tell me about the songs she had heard me sing. I just enjoyed that fine. "That Pretty Fair Maid All in a Garden." That was her favorite song.

Settlements were far apart, roads narrow and crooked, night a time for frolicking because a man was supposed to work from sun to sun, whether for himself or the other fellow. Rod Drake gives an insight into what it was like to be a lone rider on a dark road:

You'd be surprised how I done to keep awake. I used to ride lots in the night time, and sometimes I have been as long as fifteen or twenty miles from home when I'd leave these parties, and I've stayed up as high as three days and nights at a time that I'd never sleep a bit, and of course a man staying up that a way and going every night, he'll eventually get so sleepy till he'll just naturally go to sleep anywhere. I used to be a great hand to dip snuff and always carried a box in my pocket, and when I'd git so sleepy till I couldn't ride without sleeping I'd take my box of snuff out and put my finger in that snuff and put it in my eye, and it wouldn't be but about a minute till I'd go to rubbing that eye, and it'd go to running full of water, and that'd settle sleep from then on. I could make it all right and could go plumb home without any trouble.

Except for what he could remember in his own life, time for him seemed to flow without breaks. He mixed past events with present attitudes, sometimes for a tear, sometimes for a laugh, but with little sense of history, even Big Thicket history, nor of the curious juxtapositions in words like the following:

> I started one day to fair Noddingham town,
> A-riding a horse like a-walking before,
> With a little nigger drummer a-beating a drum,
> With his heels in his pockets before he could run.
> Well, the king and the queen and the company more,
> A-riding a horse like a-walking before,

With a little nigger drummer a-beating a drum,
With his heels in his pockets before he could run.

This flowing together, whether of knights and ladies, Jesse James and Cole Younger, or the everlasting love of Jesus, gives clues to the character of Big Thicket people. So did their stories of great hunts and deadly feuds. So did their rituals, one of which—a cure for third-day chills—arouses speculation on the curious, the superstitious: "Just before time for the chill to come on, the person should wrap himself tightly in a blanket, run around the house three times just as hard as he can run, run in the front door, and jump under the bed. The chill will jump into the bed and he will miss it."

In 1952 my research in the Big Thicket took on another dimension. I became director of the Oral History of Texas Oil Pioneers for the University of Texas, with the Southeast Texas fields as my special responsibility. As I had been away ten years, first as a soldier in Australia and the Philippines and then as a professor at Columbia University, I felt compelled to take a fresh look at the Thicket before I settled down to work. There were conspicuous changes in the land and the people. The Thicket appeared to have dwindled. New roads had been cut, new houses built. The people had changed even more. Young men had gone off to war and returned with memories of far-off places and different ways of living. They had returned to new advantages. Rural electrification had brought lights to houses once lit only by a light'd knot. Most of the homes had radios. Juke boxes blared in dives on what had been lonely stretches of roads. Women had been able to replace the washpot and rub board with an electric washing machine on the front porch.

By chance I met the girl who had borrowed my shoes to have her picture taken. She was now a well-groomed woman, meeting with lawyers to sign an oil lease which at the most could bring her riches, at the least, shoe money for the rest of her life. I have told the anecdote of the shoes before but not this sequel. The sequel is important as one more indication of inroads on the Big Thicket: clearing land for drilling, cutting away for roads. Whether oil was discovered or not, scars would be left.

I then went to Spindletop, where big oil first blew in, to record on tape both fact and legend from the earliest days. At Spindletop, a low mound on the coastal plain south of Beaumont, there were mineral wells that from Indian times had drawn people because of their reputed healing properties. Pattillo Higgins of Beaumont decided that minerals in the water indicated the presence of oil; that bubbles on the surface came from natural gas rising. He boxed in one of the wells, leaving an opening small enough to fit the spout of a five-gallon can.

He then filled the can with gas, capped it, and took it to Beaumont. There, in the presence of prospective speculators, he struck a match to the gas and it burned a blue flame.

The Lucas gusher, which blew in January 10, 1901, ruined the mineral wells and sent "creekologists" all over the region in search of mineral wells and bubbles on surface water. The boom, bigger than anything Pattillo Higgins ever imagined, was on. Thousands of people rushed in from Texas farms and from faraway city streets, from the oil fields of Pennsylvania and West Virginia—even a sprinkling of speculators from England and the Continent. They overflowed Beaumont and Spindletop and, after snatching up that part of the coastal plain, pushed their exploration to the edges of the Big Thicket.

At Sour Lake there were mineral springs and a mineral lake, where the Springs Hotel maintained a flourishing resort trade, where an old Negro man called "Dr. Mud" applied mud baths and prescribed the number of glasses of mineral water a day for the cure of a given ailment. Oil was discovered there in 1903 and in no time at all derricks rose among the tall pines of a virgin forest. At Batson's Prairie there were no mineral springs or lakes but after a heavy rain gas bubbled on surface water with a sound, as the people said, like ducks feeding and burned with a visible flame at night. Wells came in and within a few weeks ten thousand people lived where five families had lived before. Farther on, deeper in the Thicket, there was another mineral lake fed by a spring. There an enterprising New Yorker had set up a health resort and named it Saratoga, for Saratoga Springs. Again the surface indications were right for oil.

In a frenzy to get the oil while the getting was good, men hacked away at virgin pine and hardwood, some to be used, some to be left to rot or to burn in the fires that plagued early fields. Workers unable to afford houses or tents built shelters for themselves and their families of logs and brush and palmetto fronds. Escaping gas killed trees as tall as derricks; excess oil flowed down bayous killing as it went; salt water pumped from wells collected in low places for another kind of devastation. Fortunately, the acreage of these fields was relatively small, the duration of the booms short, measured in years, or in the

ability of the lush growth to restore itself. In those days the weapons of destruction were not so great. Men went into the woods with their axes and crosscut saws and ox-drawn wagons, or as chain tong crews who cut swaths through the growth and dug into the rooty earth deep enough to lay pipe lines.

My work soon brought me to Lance Rosier, who was living at the time with Aunt Mattie Evans at the old Vines Hotel in Saratoga. At his insistence, I interviewed her first. When the boom came to Saratoga she was a young girl living with her family out in the country. She came to the oil field with not much more than the clothes on her back and set up a boarding house in a tent, where she made enough money to be able to build the hotel in which she lived, and which she had operated for almost half a century. It was a two-story building built of rough pine lumber, boarded and stripped, with a long porch across the front. Long ago, she told me, a visitor brought her a piece of ivy which she planted near the wall. It had taken root and grown and grown and she did not have the heart to cut it back. Now it hung like a fringe along the porch and had to be pushed aside by anyone coming or going. Aunt Mattie sat in the greenish light of the porch, looking out on a yard over-crowded with mimosa seedlings—"them old Formosa trees," she called them—and talked of the rough life in the oil fields and of boomtown killings on the road in front of her hotel. The boom brought out the bad blood from the Thicket and every-where else. There was no way of telling how many died of knifings or in shoot-outs. Some names could be found in the records of violent deaths in the courthouse at Kountze—the only records left by some—but the laws were too busy to put it all down.

When she talked about the Big Thicket she became tearful. Larry Fisher had recently died of pneumonia. Some of his things were still in a room in the hotel, including many of the pictures he had made of plants and flowers. She mourned for him as a friend. She also mourned that there was no one else who could or would do the work he was doing for the Thicket. Lance agreed with her.

As Rod Drake was a key to the folk life of the Thicket, Lance Rosier was a key to the natural life. He was a small man, slight in build, light on foot, slow in movement but in no sense lethar-gic. Standing under a bay tree in the hotel yard he told me about himself. Born and raised in the Thicket, he had spent many of his boyhood days roaming through it, especially the lower part, in walking distance of Saratoga, and had come to know it well enough to work as a guide for surveyors, and, as time passed, for naturalists. In his wanderings he had come upon many kinds of plant life both strange and beautiful. With

enough education to be able to read and write, with no scientific training at all, he set out to identify these plants. Help had to come from outside. He sent samples of leaf, flower, and stem to botanists in universities—as far away as Cornell—and asked for identification. When the names came back, though he had no Latin, he memorized them. As the years passed, as he guided naturalists and others through the botanically rich parts of the Thicket, Lance became a remarkable source of information, accurate and detailed and stored only in his memory. By the time I came to him, his reputation as a guide was well established. He could guide to where wild orchids grew, or as easily to an egret rookery or where a bear had left claw marks on a tree.

In less than an afternoon, while we went around the old Saratoga field from the remnants of the mineral lake where the discovery well had come in to the edges where vegetation was covering rotting derricks and rusting pipes, Lance was able to tell me and show me why the Big Thicket is of unique interest to naturalists. It has often been called "The Biological Crossroads of North America," and with good reason. Here the flora and fauna of North and South, East and West mingle and intermingle. Northern maples and beeches stand not too great a distance from cypress and Southern magnolias. American hollies grow large; orchids bloom among Northern ferns; mesquite and tumbleweed, plants of the Western desert, survive where the annual rainfall averages sixty inches. On a major flyway, the Big Thicket is a stopping place for many birds in passage as well as home to a wide variety. Beavers build dams; an occasional coyote yips in the night.

When the subject of conservation came up, our talk turned to Roy Bedichek, himself a self-taught ornithologist, author of *Adventures with a Texas Naturalist*. Lance knew of him and his efforts at saving the whooping crane. He might be willing to join the fight to save the Big Thicket. I wanted Bedi to know the Big Thicket. Even more, I wanted him to know Lance.

Four years passed before the meeting took place. It was May, a good time to travel Texas roads, and Bedi, though seventy-two, was as expectant as a schoolboy at the prospect of new adventures. He had built up a dream, a hope: somewhere in the Big Thicket he would see an ivory-billed woodpecker. Hope turned to something like expectation after we crossed the Trinity River and came to a stretch of road cut through tall trees and lush undergrowth. I took the wheel; he sat with his binoculars ready, his eyes scanning the treetops. After a time, in an open space, he saw an albino dove on a fence post by the road. Farther along, in woods again, we saw a woodpecker big as a crow fly across the gap of green cut by the road.

"Pileated," Bedi said, disappointment in his voice.

We drove on to Kountze and put up at the Carricker Hotel.

It was late afternoon when Bedi and Lance met, when the sun was aslant and shadows were beginning to create a sense of the unreal, the mysterious in the close-growing thickets. In the way they greeted each other I knew how right I had been to bring them together, the highly sophisticated university man and the unsophisticated woodsman, both searchers for nature's secrets. Within an hour they were bent over a coral snake killed by a car on the road, noting its size and how the rainbow rings were beginning to dull, talking about its habits, Bedi from what he had learned in books, Lance from his own observations.

"He's a rare bird," Bedi said of Lance when we were back at the Carricker.

For three full days Lance showed us some of his favorite parts of the Big Thicket, starting with the Old Bragg Road, where walls of trees—pines and hardwoods—still showed what road and railroad builders encountered in the early days; where at night mysterious lights, gaseous or whatever, have fired local imaginations until it is called "The Ghost Road." To the farther places—Pine Island Bayou, Honey Island, Thicket—we went in the pickup. To others, we walked, making slow progress be-

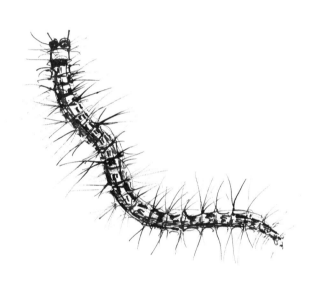

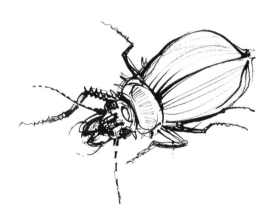

cause there were so many things for Lance to show, so many things for Bedi to see. The rarest of all, because the ivory-bill never showed himself, was a flock of roseate spoonbills hidden in a spot that only Lance seemed to know.

Once on a dim trail they came upon a copperhead stretched out in dappled shade, undisturbed by their approach. Again they compared notes on color and size and habits. My instinct was to beat any copperhead into the ground with a stick, but not theirs. They studied this one until it woke. Then they stood back and watched it glide out of sight in the underbrush.

Early on our last morning Lance took us out toward Little Pine Island Bayou to show us what the oil field had done. We drove on an old road through second-growth pine and hardwood and then came to a place where nothing grew. In the middle of a stretch of barren sand there was a shallow lake perhaps half a mile across, with here and there the branches of dead trees gray-black against the bright blue sky. On the branches perched white egrets like giant flowers in a surrealistic garden. The whole area smelled of brackish water and rotting vegetation. Lance explained. This was a salt water run off from oil well pumpings. Wherever this water collected—in bayou, creek, or pond—the effect was the same—the destruction of still another part of the Big Thicket.

Lance had made his point clear: At the rate it was being ravaged, the Thicket would soon belong entirely to legend. That night Bedichek and I went to see R. E. Jackson, president of the East Texas Big Thicket Association, at his home in Silsbee to learn what was being done, what could be done to save it. We arrived at first dark, when lights had to be turned on in the living room for the men to see each other as they talked.

Jackson did most of the talking. Seemingly a quiet, unassuming man at first, he fired up as the talk turned to conservation. As a railroad conductor he had seen the parts of the Thicket crossed by railroads in all seasons, at all hours, day or night; he had hiked parts that seemed impenetrable to many; he controlled land there; he had been a leader of the Association since it was founded in 1927.

As he talked he ranged over a hundred years of Big Thicket history, from the hackings at it by hand to the stripping by machine—from the settlers taking what they needed to the lumber companies cutting over thousands of acres and floating logs down the river to sawmills and markets. The hand had been destructive, the machine infinitely more so. The individual might be reasoned with but not the company.

Patterns of frustration emerged as he recounted the efforts for thirty years to create a Big Thicket National Park, efforts that were on again, off again while the lumber companies continued to cut and developers were beginning to build homes for paradise living, while members of the East Texas Big Thicket Association were too divided to carry on an effective fight.

Time came for us to go. We left his home that night, the Big Thicket the next morning, saddened and perplexed. The whooping crane was being saved but it never had the price tag that was attached to the Big Thicket, and it provided a single dramatic image—impossible to find in acres and miles of swamps and streams, bayous and baygalls, in the myriad of impressions that make up the Big Thicket.

In 1971 I met Michael Frary, whose paintings are the substance of this book, whose love affair with the Big Thicket is as fresh and as abiding as any I have encountered. A native Californian, a painter of broad attainments, Frary was almost entirely a stranger to the kind of scenes he found in the Big Thicket when he came in 1966. Fortunately, he had Lance Rosier as guide and Dempsie Henley, author of *The Murder of Silence*, as host—both natives. Of Lance and their first meeting Frary says:

We went to Saratoga where we met Lance. All he did to prepare for the four-day camping trip was to put on his old brown hat and say, "Let's go." He directed us to an isolated spot on Menard Creek near Whoop and Holler. After helping to set up camp, which consisted of one small tent and folding cots for everyone, I went off some distance and started two water colors.

When I returned it was practically dark and everyone was sitting by the fire. Lance was explaining the sounds of the approaching night. He related each sound to a specific insect or animal and told something of interest about each one. As he did this, I began to "see" into the forest even thought it was dark. The Thicket began to open up and take on a life of its own. Later on Lance identified smells and tastes in the same manner. He loved the Thicket with all of his senses.

Lance took us to see fields of carnivorous plants, four or five different varieties. He showed us where bears had scratched the bark on trees; he showed us beaver dams, "bee" trees, sassafras trees, iron wood, huge magnolias, biggest holly tree in the world, sweet gums —ten feet in diameter—rattan and wild grape vines hanging from limbs of trees one hundred feet above the ground. Lance identified with every living thing in the Thicket. He was the St. Francis of the Big Thicket.

Even the least sensitive traveler in the Thicket, seeing patterns of color and shape, of light and shadow on trunk or vine, on flower or leaf, may exclaim, "That's as pretty as a picture." Almost since the beginning of photography, camera experts have tried to catch parts of the Thicket that would faithfully render a sense of the whole. Michael Frary, with the special gift of the painter, has captured the mystery and uniqueness of the land in impressions that, though not always readily recog-

nizable in the details, more truthfully represent the Thicket than photographs ever could. Again and again under his brush, patterns emerge, sometimes harsh, sometimes soft, as if he had seen the Thicket as a giant tapestry, too broad for the eye to comprehend—so broad that it has to be taken a patch at a time and brought close for intense scrutiny.

Frary's first trip to the Big Thicket was followed by others:

Dempsie generously loaned me his lake house near Rye on at least five painting trips. One time I spent two weeks by myself there. I would drive out on different routes every morning in Dempsie's four-wheel-drive jeep and stop and paint whatever interested me. Then usually I would come back about one o'clock, paint inside during the hottest part of the day, go out about five, draw or paint until dark, come back, have something to eat, and paint until sometimes two or three in the morning from memory and impressions I had received during the day. This was a very productive period for me and it was only possible because of Dempsie's hospitality and generosity.

I guess my favorite spots are the Alabama-Coushatta Indian Reservation, the Pine Island Bayou, the banks of the Trinity and some "secret" places along Menard Creek.

Frary says that he painted what interested him. The seventy-two paintings in this book are more concerned with the scenes of the Big Thicket than with its people. He believes that people began ruining the Thicket when they first entered and have almost succeeded in destroying it. There are more pictures of birds than of buildings, though the buildings are evocative of a way of life, especially those of the early period of settlement. One is tempted to linger longest over the less-defined scenes, the impressionistic recordings of "secret places," whether they came from recesses deep in the Big Thicket or from recesses deep in the artist's mind.

Dempsie Henley, in *The Murder of Silence*, updated to 1970, recounts fully, sometimes with irony, sometimes with bitterness, the long struggle to create a Big Thicket National Park, or Monument—a struggle that in forty years has enlisted on one side or the other financiers, politicians, conservationists, and countless Thicket lovers strong in will but weak in power. The East Texas Big Thicket Association and R. E. Jackson passed from the scene, to be succeeded by the Big Thicket Association of Texas, with Dempsie Henley as president. New blood, new projects, such as the Big Thicket Museum, but the basic conflict remains the same: how much of the Thicket will belong to timbering and other big financial interests for exploitation, how much to the people—parts to be enjoyed, parts to be left alone for the kind of natural recycling that has gone on for ages.

As early as 1938 a study team for the National Park Service

recommended that a part of the region be set aside for preservation and incorporated in the National Park system. In 1965 the Park Service again recommended in favor of a park. In 1966, after further study, it recommended the preservation of nine representative "specimen areas," the "string of pearls." These widely dispersed tracts, unconnected by any kind of corridors, total 35,000 acres. This recommendation pleased the lumber companies but not the conservationists. In the meantime, however, while these studies were in progress, Senator Ralph Yarborough, on the side of the conservationists, was presenting a bill before the Senate that would establish a Big Thicket National Park not to exceed 75,000 acres. This bill was read and laid aside to await the development of a bill in the House.

In the years since, the conflict has gone on, while the Big Thicket is rapidly disappearing, some say at the rate of fifty acres a day. Of the countless business organizations and individuals hacking away at the Big Thicket, the timber-paper industry is the major destroyer. Through its highly organized, well-funded Texas Forestry Association, it can lobby in Austin and Washington, or through speakers present its point of view to garden clubs or other interested groups. The point of view can be presented with a certain reasonableness: that the Big Thicket has already been cut over till it is no more than a "romantic state of mind"; that most of the specimens of plant and animal life found there may also be found elsewhere; that the reforestation program they have in force is sound both commercially and ecologically. They can claim in fact that they have actually regrown the Thicket. Ecologists on the other hand point out that such tree farming requires clearing the land of hardwoods by the use of herbicides, bulldozing, and plowing, and then planting pine seedlings row on row. This kind of reforestation eliminates natural recovery and is likely to create a biological desert.

The Texas Forestry Association has long had a standing offer to set aside 35,000 acres, the "string of pearls" tracts, for preservation. More recently, the Association has been willing to discuss a compromise through which they would increase their offer to as much as 82,000 acres by trading off for federally owned lands farther north in East Texas, Their second offer may be too late to aid them in maintaining their position of preference. Saving the Big Thicket is no longer a Texas interest alone. Such national voices as the Sierra Club, the *New York Times*, *The National Observer*, and the *Chicago Tribune* are making themselves heard. Dr. Thomas Eisner, biologist at Cornell University, has organized a group of scientists called the Ad Hoc Committee to Save the Big Thicket. Their chief thrust,

and that of many lesser voices around the country, is to persuade the United States government to save at least 200,000 acres of the Big Thicket.

Meanwhile, there has been some progress in Washington. Senator Yarborough's bill passed the Senate but died in the House Interior Committee, partially because the National Park Service, instead of pushing for passage, asked for delays in order that more studies of boundaries and other problems might be made. At present Representative Robert Eckhardt has a bill before the house which would create a Big Thicket National Park not to exceed 100,000 acres. Amended from the original stipulation of 191,000 acres, it has the advantage that it suggests specific boundaries. It includes the "string of pearls" tracts, some additional tracts to be purchased from timber companies, and connecting corridors on major waterways: Pine Island Bayou, Village Creek, the Neches River, and others. A park of this extent including these areas would be ecologically acceptable and, in spite of intense opposition from the timber-paper industry, politically feasible if concerted pressure can be brought to bear in Washington.

Whatever the outcome of these confrontations, future generations will have cause to be grateful to Michael Frary for his Big Thicket paintings. Not all can be preserved. Scenes even from his "secret places" will go, bulldozed up, shredded up, paved over—streams straightened till they would make no sense to an alligator or a "mud turkle," familiar patterns of land and life obliterated for the sake of development houses, for precious pines planted row on row waiting for the time when a computer will say they are ready to be cut for the paper pulp mill.

WILLIAM A. OWENS

PLATES

Cypress trees and knees on Boggy Creek

Slave Lake

Worm-eaten cypress on Bad Luck Creek

Tangles of growth on Steep Bank Creek

Concord Baptist Church, near Rye, founded in 1848; Sam Houston attended services here.

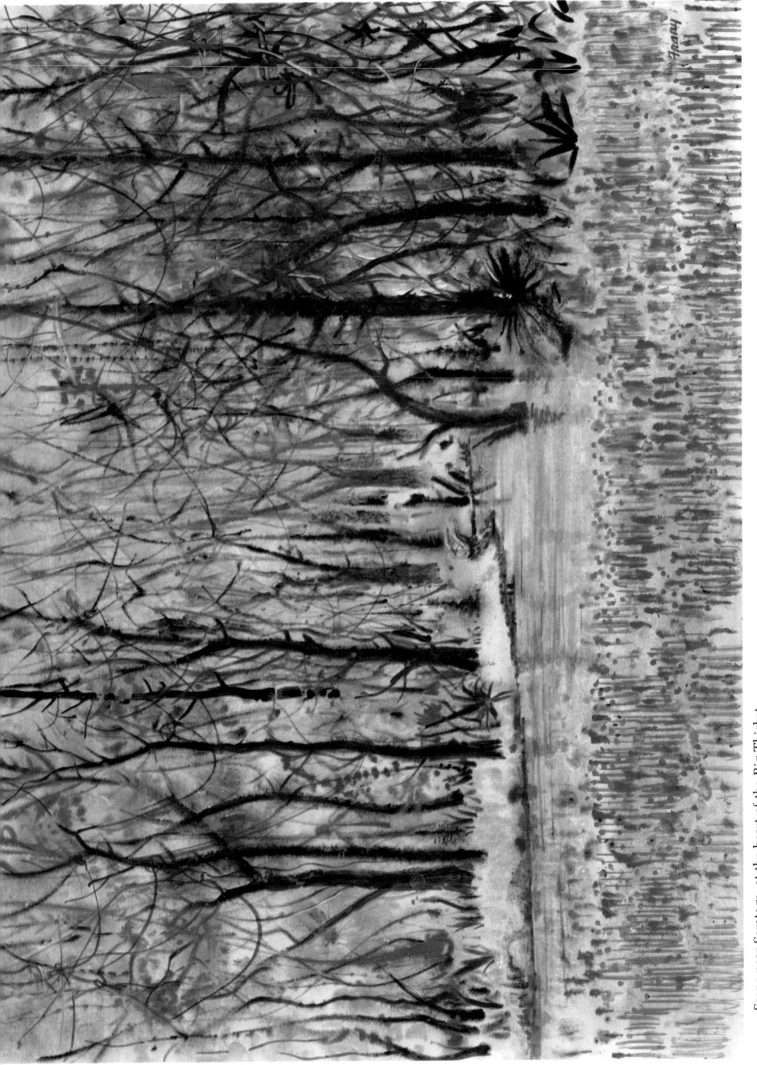

Scene near Saratoga, at the heart of the Big Thicket

47

Patterns of trees and leaves

Sluggish brown water in Pine Island Bayou

49

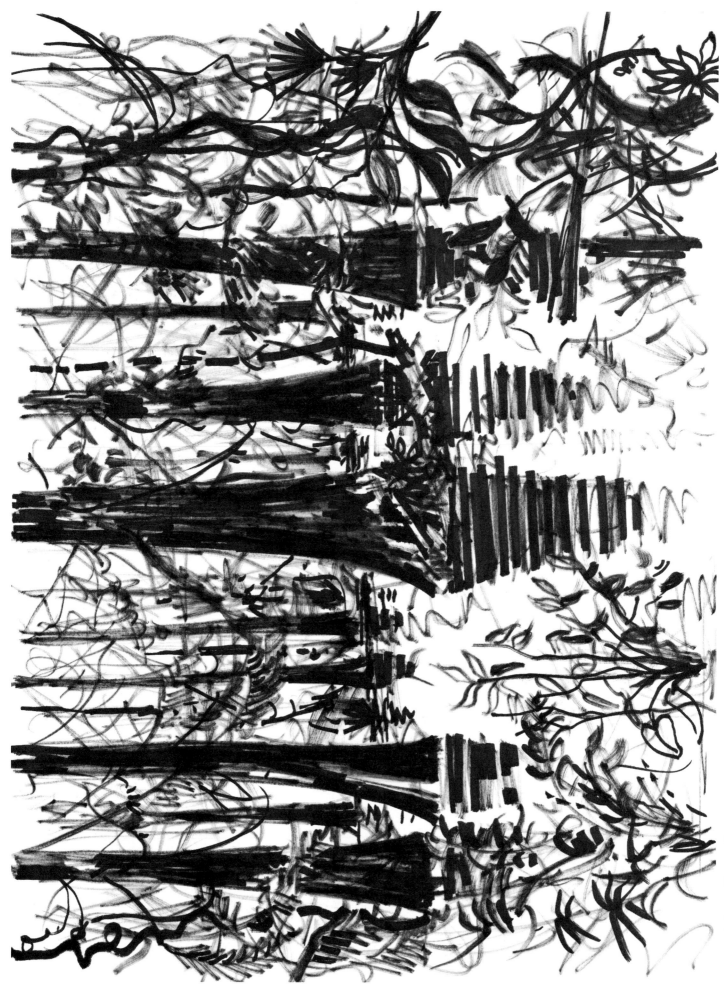

A baygall near Romayer

Grape vines swinging from a tall sweet gum on Dempsie's island

Palmettos by the water, Daniel's Plantation Ranch

Trinity water cutting into a sandy bank

53

Design of leaves and briars

Pattern of trees and flowers at Honey Island

Logging road near Whoop and Holler

Time of the loon

Morning over Menard Creek

Trinity River above the coastal plain

Cypress trees and creek water

Nature in infinite variety

Sunlight reaching deep into a baygall

Trinity River sands and bluffs and cattle coming down to drink

Rough country near the Kaiser Burnout

Frany

An edge of Batson's Prairie

Vines as thick as your leg

Paths quickly overgrown

Two young trees

Home of the egret

Canopy of oaks and magnolias above mayhaw patches

Mysterious night on Black Land Slough

71

Morning light on the brown water of Bad Luck Creek

House where Dempsie Henley was raised

Union Wells Creek

Natural association: birds, bees, flowers, trees

75

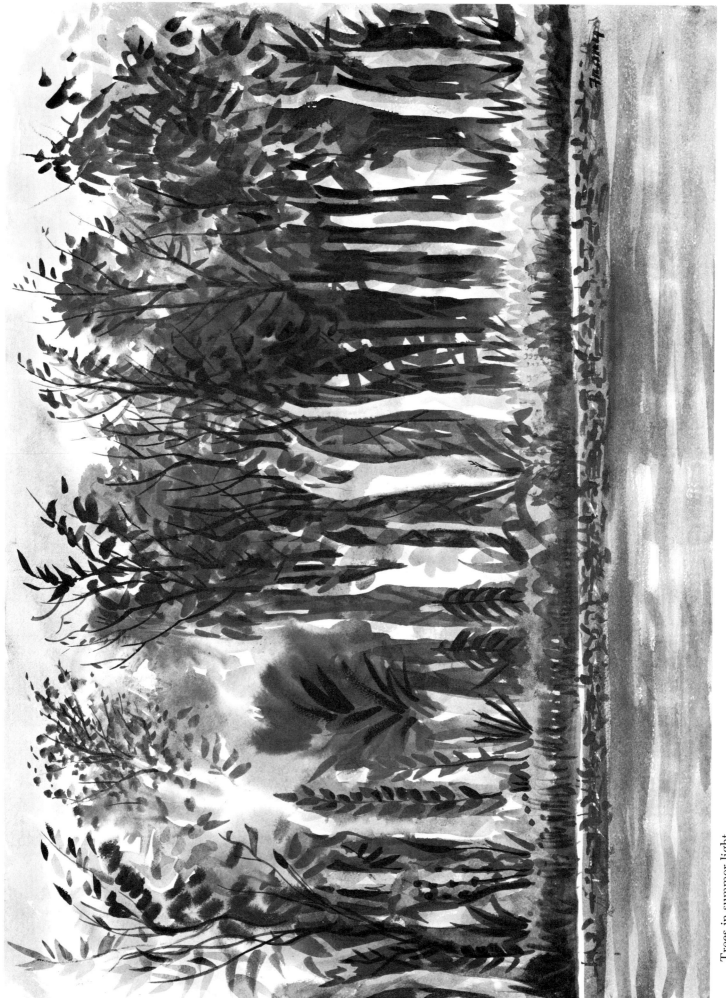

Trees in summer light

Pintails in flight

Vines, from wild grape to poison ivy

Waterfall—rare in the Thicket, where water runs slow as time

79

Big Thicket house abandoned to egrets

Dempsie Henley's island in the Trinity

NEOX FLORA

82

Slave Lake tapestry

On Ten Mile Gully

Log road near the Alabama-Coushatta Reservation

Island in the Trinity

Egrets and white herons

Small baygall on Cypress Creek

Logging road near Menard Creek

Slave Lake near Horseshoe Bend

Aspect of leaves

Tangle of vines

Egrets in a sunny glade

Black Creek mystery

Vines, vines, vines—stretchberry and muscadine, smilax and rattan

Trinity River sand bar

Old tree, Alabama-Coushatta Reservation

White trees, dark water

Unusual colors, shapes, textures

Horseshoe Bend Lake at dusk

Oak near Long King's Village

Mayhaw slough

Reflections

Giant live oak near Rye

Carnivorous pitcher plants with buckeye in bloom

Solitary crane in slough

The sound of water

Where moccasins sun on low-hanging branches

Back to the nest

Does the ivory-bill still live in the Thicket?

Sun and shade

Ghost road, Saratoga to Bragg